SELECTED POEMS

C. J. Stevens

32769027

Published by John Wade, Publisher
P.O. Box 303, Phillips, Maine 04966

Library of Congress Cataloging in Publication Data
Selected Poems # 95-60291

ISBN # 1-882425-04-9 cloth
ISBN # 1-882425-05-7 paperback

First Edition
Printed in the United States of America

These poems are for Stella

ACKNOWLEDGMENTS

These poems have been selected from three previous books of poetry: *Beginnings and Other Poems*, 1989; *Circling at the Chain's Length*, 1991; and *Hang-Ups*, 1993.

I thank the editors of the following publications in which most of these poems first appeared: *Aldebaran, American Weave, Ann Arbor Review, Ante, The Antigonish Review (Canada), Apostrophe, Apple, Aspect, Aspect Magazine, Barataria, The Barat Review, Butt, The Cambridge Review* (England), *The Carleton Miscellany, Casaba, The Chowder Review, Circus Maximus, College English, Colorado State Review, The Colorado Quarterly, Confrontation, Connecticut Fireside, El Corno Emplumado* (Mexico), *The Crescent, The Cresset* (Canada), *Cronopios, Descant, Discourse, Empty Belly, Etc., The Expatriate Review, The Far Point* (Canada), *The Fiddlehead* (Canada), *Film Quarterly, Folio, Forum, The Free South Review, Handsel, Hanging Loose, Harrison Street Review, Hierophant, Hollow Spring Review, Hyacinths and Biscuits, Icarus, Jam To-Day, Jeopardy, Kansas Magazine, Kansas Quarterly, The Laurel Review, Lip Service, The Literary Review, The Little Review, Maelstrom, The Midwest Quarterly, Mississippi Valley Review, Modern Age, Mountain Summer, The Nation, New: American & Canadian Poetry, New Frontiers* (England), *New Mexico Quarterly, Northeast Journal, Ore* (England), *The Panhandler, Peace and Freedom* (England), *Pennine Platform* (England), *Poem, The Poetry Bag, Poetry Forum, Poetry Now, Poetry Nottingham* (England), *The Post Crescent, Prairie Schooner, Prisms International* (Canada), *Red Cedar Review, Road Apple Review, Screen Door Review, The Small Pond, The Smith, South Coast Poetry Journal, Stoney Lonesome, Stride* (England), *Twigs* (Canada), *Urthkin, La Voix des Poétes* (France), *West Branch, West Coast Review, Wind, The Windless Orchard*, and *Wormwood Review*.

Many of these poems have appeared in collections with the following presses: *The Crossing Press, Icarus Press, Juniper Press, Poet & Printer* (London), *and Sparrow Press.*

"Cabin Fever" was published as a postcard poem by *Blue Crow Press,* and *"The Barn"* as *Phoenix* Broadsheet *No. 317* (England).

Further acknowledgments are made to the publishers of these anthologies and textbooks: "Flowering After Frost," *Brandon Press*; "For The Love of Cats," *The Crossing Press*; "Fundamental English," *Gjellerup* (Denmark); "Man In the Poetic Mode," Books 1 & 6, *McDougal, Littell & Company*; "31 New American Poets," *Hill & Wang, Inc.;* "Themes In Poetry and Song," *McGraw-Hill Book Company*; "New Maine Writing," *Maine NESPA;* "An Anthology of Magazine Verse," *Monitor Book Company*; "An Anthology of Contemporary American Poetry," *Peace & Pieces*; "Junior Voices," *Penguin Books Ltd.*; "World Literature," *USIA* (Poland); "It's Only A Movie," "The Heart of the Matter," and "Nova: Anthology of Literary Types," *Prentice-Hall, Inc*; "Real World English," *Scholastic Book Services*; "28 Poems," *Sumac Press*; and "Aspect Anthology," *Zephyr Press.*

CONTENTS

SELECTED POEMS

HOMETOWN

Years later, you visit the town
of your childhood and find
the fields and woods are
parking lots and streets. Your hide-
and-seek pasture has become
a trailer park. A turnpike splits
your old neighborhood. All afternoon
you prowl the sidewalks for one
remembered face. Nobody you know
passes you. The human race
has forgotten World War II
and the Great Depression. Strangers
crowd the boulevards, and the fumes
from engines dirty the snow. Even
the oaks in the square have been pulled
from the earth—they've been replaced
with boxes of plastic geraniums.
Tenements rise like fungus
along the hillside. You soon
get lost. Not one person stops
when you ask directions. At dusk,
a cop on his beat becomes
suspicious. He shakes you down.
Your only alibi: you've come to see
your hometown. But the cop
is young and inexperienced. He has
no use for aliens and old men
who lie. You keep telling him
how the world was once. He shakes his head,
probes you with his stick. He tells you
to get out of his town and to be quick.

WALKING HOME BEFORE SUNRISE

The spruce jaws of entrances
yawn while the hooked moon
fishes on the horizon for fat clouds,
and the startled prehistoric eye
of a window blinks at a car light.
The nailed stars come loose
from the Milky Way as a puddle
of daylight drenches the miniature elms
and smeared leaves of distant hills.
I begin to sense the long unwinding
of events. I can imagine
the closed throat of a mountain
as it chokes on the bones
of buffalo and elk; gnawed bones
that a tribesman left when he
went out to kill. Further back,
the brontosaurus stretches into a cathedral
as it lifts its head. There is an emptiness
I cannot explain when the streets
have no people. There is only
the wind stalking the simpering trees.
Time begins to rewind as I walk home.

THE SMELL OF WOOD

There's something to think about
when you lay your head in the grass
and the smell of dry sticks
boned in the turf reminds you
of kindling and a sharp axe.
It's then your sense of smell
brings back the man who looks
like you, but is a young
rendition—straighter, with axe
poised and muscles hard
as stove wood. You stand back;
you watch. His legs break from
their oak stance, and a bolt
of steel divides a block
of beech. You smell blood
as the sap jewels up
from the cramped veins and the smell
takes you back with your head
in the grass and you're holding
a dry stick. An object for
attention. Something to smell.

THE FAMILIAR

How quickly, easily
my regard for the familiar deepens
when I look at objects I have kept
for no known reasons: quartz
from a forgotten quarry, a ballpoint pen
with stiffening ink, and even that one
unmatched button found among my handkerchiefs.
I have come to think of them as preparations;
they are my reaching out to comprehend
what I still am after having used them.
Meanwhile through disuse and neglect
they grow in significance
and I can no longer be free of them.
Now, with their surfaces and contours
dulled with dust, their purposes gone,
I pick them up one by one—
still aware I am of the familiarity gained
and the objectivity lost.

THE ASCENT

I tell you man must
burn his fingers—touch
the sun. He must drill
his eyes with stars, and when
he cracks open the woman comes.
She will wrap the bandage.
The salve of her hands will ease
his mind. He'll think: man
is everywhere—at the woman's
thigh, on the nipple's top—
and he'll dream-dream-dream
from the darkest pit. He won't
look down. He can't. The plant
of his spine shoots up-up—
all the way. At the top
he doesn't stop thinking of planets
and stars. He'll still feel
her hands salving the sores.
There's always the going up
to make him dizzy, almost
crazy, and he loves it.

SPRING PLANS

The long grass
with its tanned
thighs rubs against
the woodshed.

Leaves
hug the waterspout,
then swarm to
the frog pond.

Late last fall
a backhoe slit
the throat of dirt
where mustard trampled
the oregano.

Tomorrow
I'm going to burn
the grass, string
a clothesline, and build
a birdhouse.

I'll be
out there when the swallows
return. I've got
spring plans.

MAY

The sun begins to climb
its new trellis of leaves
and the last thread of snow
becomes a stitch of mildew
under the trees. Dandelions
tatter the lawn and the purple
lungs of lilacs sweeten
the bush. The birds come back
as the mud roads dry
and a gown of dust covers
the roadside brush. Between
the first torn cry of a bull-
frog's speech and the beacon
of a firefly the mosquitoes
start their engines and the grass
lengthens. Twilight crayons
a window and the wind
unwinds its unseen skeins.
At dawn, a woodpecker opens
a sore on the flexed arm
of an elm. Another day
begins. It won't
be long before butterflies
blossom into flight.

CHARCOALS

If we erase
a few light lines
around the eyes
and charcoal in
a spiderweb
of wrinkles, we
get the faces
right but not the
people.

      And grief
isn't easy.
We charcoal in
a tear; rub out
an eyebrow and
an ear—oh no,
oh no, we can't
begin to make
our miseries
that clear. It just
wouldn't do. Oh
no.

      And as we
often are is
most difficult
of all—we are
true distortions
pinned to a wall.
Erase and re-
erase, we can't

begin to sketch
the pleasure found
behind the face.
Oh no. We are
comics scissored
from great cartoons.

FINGERS

They are often
clumsy, seldom
expert. They go
wherever we
go—little slaves
at work. Each leaves
a footprint of
its own, a trail
of grime jeweled
with sweat. No two
alike, they come
to attention
in a handshake
and bow and scrape
whenever they
mine the soft caves
of our pockets
for change. They get
excited when
we hesitate.
Each wears a beard
of dirt but keeps
a shiny face.
They make love to
axes and hoes
and even chase
the written word.
They risk their lives
on saws, and when
the cut is deep

and bood begins
to run we wrap
them gently in
a cloud of gauze
and let them sleep.

NOON

Now, the clocks hold up their arms. Since dawn, no moisture.
The sun plunders the rich maze of the earth, and our bodies
swelter under the sticky shade of trees. A phone
wire flashes into mirages and out again: a streak
of lonely silver, running slenderly to the sea,
escaping the shimmer of dancing towns. Now, the leak
of seconds. The clocks obey the pulling sun and rasp
in unison. Shadows embroider a charred bush.
Soon, the tilted day will atone our suffering.
But we burn with our straight fevers like the shadowless plants.

CHAIRS

There are five silent chairs in this room.
They are dusty and empty and lonesome for people.
What the first one needs is loving attention—someone
with strong hands to push her rungs
into place. If she were mine,
I would tighten her with some glue
and rock with her as only lovers can do.
If I had the time, I would sit on the lap
of the second one and sigh myself to sleep.
She looks so sensual with that hem
of sunlight stitched across the soft breast
of her pillow. The third one is a small fellow
with a stiff back. The plump bottom
of a maiden would make him seem less formal.
He is the only male, and his loneliness is complete.
I'm tempted to throw my jacket over his knobby shoulders.
The fourth one is more worn and experienced
than the first three. If I had this one,
I would tell her that she is still beautiful
in her gown of pink burlap with smudges of grease
and how sweetly she still sings when she creaks.
Last, but more imposing than the other four,
is the bosomy old sofa. She stretches out
in all her upholstered splendor. A fat period piece
of a wild era. If I didn't have to leave,
I would scrape loose her cat hairs and telltale stains
and let her gossipy old springs fill this room with chatter.

WORDS

You find yourself writing them,
but words get jammed. They can
come out fragmented. Unreal.
The words you write must chase your hand.
They can be crushed from the throat,
brushed past the lips. But if you don't
rise to meet words, they slip
awkwardly back. They become deadweights.
Then you carry them around like stones.
If they are to move, you must roll them up.
You let them inflate like balloons,
and there must be enough helium
to lift you off your feet. Nobody knows
if a word will stir you awake or let you down.

LANDFILL

The bulldozers have fasted all morning
while the coughing trucks back up to dump
their cargoes of phlegm into the slit throat
of the faceless hill. The earth takes in
its nourishment for the unborn grass and trees,
and the wind chokes on a mound of disfigured vegetables
as an empty truck grinds out of neutral and leaves.
There must be a protein burial every other day.
It's time now for the ritual of dirt on dirt;
time for the starving bulldozers to begin work.
The pulses of machines flutter with the rich blood
of gasoline. Up and down the wide cut
of the landscape, a dirge of engines can be heard.
All afternoon these screaming mourners pace back and forth
among the metal skeletons and cardboard corpses
until the bones of all the cadavers are crushed
by the heavy tread of Caterpillars. The open mouth
of the grave fills. The dead are stacked upon the dead.
By nightfall only a few pieces of broken glass
will be seen on the new skin of the landfill.
The glass will shine like pins in the moonlight.
The earth is ready now to nourish its unborn grass,
and the wind is restless as it prowls for trees.

THE BARN

The universe
is just the place
to get lost in.
A big old barn.
Dark. Forsaken.
It took courage
to build that one.
And the lumber!
Just think of it.
All those black boards
and star-shaped nails.

BEGINNINGS

You were led into the parking lot behind Woolworth's
when the midnight world was bandaged with snow
and the veins in the thermometers were almost bloodless.
Maybe it was after the picture show, probably
your first time ever with him or any man.
You get in, slump on the back seat of his Buick.
The door slams behind him. He begins
by whistling some new hit tune of the nineteen twenties
while your breasts pillow his head. Then fingers burrow into
buttonholes until your coat loosens. A stir in the dark
as he licks your hand. You try to shift the weight
of his back from your lap, try to sit straight and ladylike.
But he is strong and determined as he turns and presses you down.
His lips nibble at your chin, and the juicy meat
of his mouth smells of gin as his tongue races
across your tongue. Your neck stiffens as his fingers
scurry like trapped rodents along your spine.
You sob, cry out, ask him to stop. He is no longer
kind and sensitive, he becomes ravenous, kisses gnaw
at your throat, a knee grinds into your thigh.
You twist for breath, and he pulls at your dress
until it rips. But you are still innocent—enough
to hope, even to pretend. You quickly reach out
to calm him, coax him to be gentle, beg him to wait.
Your words excite him, your fears arouse his need to hurt.
Nails claw at your midriff, a snarl builds in his throat.
Now he is pushing and slapping. He must take you,
he must tame you for the loveless years to come.
You wait expectantly, you are confused and afraid.
Afterwards, you know the cold threat of his hands.
He will tear at you, strip you bare. And I was born.

GREAT-UNCLE CROWELL

Great-uncle Crowell slapped my face
when my marble of spittle rolled down his vest:
I was perched on the sweet-apple bough
of my mother's knee; Crowell was hooked
like a thorn to a cushion of his settee
that stood in the shade of this apple tree.

When one is five, one is surprised
that grown-ups are capable of storms—
the mountainous thunder of Crowell's voice,
and lightning splintering the knotted
pupils of my mother's eyes.

                  And then
my uncle, who had no place to go,
took cot and bowl and a soiled vest
and fled. He went to the barn to live.
"The final insult," my mother said.
But I thought of the drooling cows; thought
of the wind slapping the faceless trees.

JIGSAW

Good as gold, fine
as silk: two clichés
from the days when the stoves
had nickel-plated fronts
and Model A's would stall
like mules. And I remember
nights of silver after
the first snow; remember
the smell of chive, clove;
taste the checkerberry
on a sugared spoon.
It runs together: pail
after pail of water
down that timeless river.
The child discovers, the man
remembers, and nothing is lost.
Most of the gold and silk:
clichés from a childhood
that somehow fit together.
I'm still finding pieces.
I'm still picking them up.

UNCLE ED

A ragged quilt upon the feather tick,
a nosebleed spray of blossoms
on the cracked wallpaper, and the smell
of creosote from the chimney
in that Maine bedroom in August.

Then the mangy-dog appearance
of Uncle Ed covered with rags
upon that iron-posted bed.
I stand at the door and watch him slide
the log of his arm to the floor,
rap his pipe on the wet lip of the pot.

The dying man decides for himself
why the ashes divide like cells
and sink. He compares the yellow waste
with the waste of August-day light.
Then he pulls the log back to suck
the black teat until it drains.

UPSTAIRS

I went upstairs
to watch it move.
I kept it there
under some clothes
in a small box.
It felt so warm
when I held it.
Then I dropped it.
It didn't move
for a long time,
and the next day
when I touched it,
it felt funny.
It wouldn't crawl.
It wasn't warm.
Something was bad
inside. I knew
it wasn't mine
the way it was.
It's still up there.
I don't want it
because it's cold.
I won't go near.
I stay downstairs.
It's warm down here,
and I'm happy.

THE CLOTHESLINE

In the backyard
I can see the cloth lungs
of my shirt suck in
the scoured wind. There is something
out there I have never been able
to slip on and button
up to my chin.

When I
was ten I nearly got
it on. I had been keeping
in step with the rinsed step
of underwear. One light-
footed spin, and I would
have swung with the starched bones
along the line.

Since then
I have become suspicious
of weights and measurements.
I take my wooden walks,
and I feel pinned whenever
I watch the handkerchief
behavior of birds; whenever
I study the weather for signs
of a high wind.

1939

My parents stayed up late the year that Poland fell
they talked about the weather, the neighborhood, and the nation
but never about the commentators' predictions
it was a time of aggravation and apprehension
so many dreams were temporarily suspended
promises were made and broken without explanations
I played football in the backyard until dark
and my parents spun the radio dial like a top
bravery and honor were words we all took for granted
so many people I knew appeared strange and uncertain
the neighborhood seemed smaller as the oceans narrowed
flags were unfurled and the national anthem repeated
we all hated Hitler—everyone was patriotic
the cut moon scythed the cornfields and the ground stiffened
the leaves curled like banners, fell red and lifeless
this was the year cartography had no meaning
my loathsome geography book was soon outdated
the playgrounds and back lots were all deserted
goblins and ghosts were prowling the dark stables
everyone felt the impossible would soon happen
the only certainty I knew was my stamp collection
and all that summer, into the chill of autumn
my parents stayed up late—talking, talking.

WHEN THERE IS NO PLACE TO GO

When there is
no place to go
to be lonely, when I
can't hide in my own house
or scare the people outside
with the sallow complexion
of a pushed drape, when strangers
seep through the cracks
of my senses, when the world
rattles like a garbage can
at dawn, when I can't
think or lie down or sit still,
when I'm pressed against
the damp walls and smeared
into the woodwork
like paint, it's then,
and only then, I recall
the inscrutable black eyes
of empty houses taunting
an empty street; back when
there were only a few people
and the world was
big and haunted.

SNAPSHOT

father and son are caught in a backyard snapshot
I must have been eighteen, my father forty-eight
I'm obviously posing—a soldier home on furlough
I don't like my pompous stance, my gentlemanly grin:
head up, shoulders squared, cigarette pointing at the camera
I'm probably thinking how old my father looked then
I wonder why he stands there looking so pleased?
he's smiling—maybe he sees himself in me
maybe he's trying to think of a joke, to say something obscene
he looks so squashed in his suit, an aging ice cream man
his bow tie clings to his throat like an injured butterfly
the sleeves of his coat are penciled with thick lines
his trousers ride on the high slope of his paunch
maybe he wants to crawl into the lens to remember
but I, I'm waiting for the shutter to wink knowingly
I'm eighteen, the world is focused on me, never my father
I don't like what I'm doing with my other hand
will it touch the money he gave me? will it smooth his coat?
father and son, side by side, the two of us together
he showing his pride, I hiding my shame

THE CENTURIES OF PEASANT BLOOD IN ME

The centuries of peasant blood in me,
down to the premises of black nails,
are marvelously busy this bright morning
as I straddle the trench, feeling the flood
of irrigational red to the packed cells
that stack my shoulders in two piles of earth.
Hands, old as my people, grip the spade.
If the landscape changes, the flesh remains:
sturdy as the love of ancient labor;
solid as the ground where the spade falls.

THINKING ABOUT MY FATHER

Because I haven't the courage
to say *yes* when you perversely
remind me that you are slowly
dying, because I can't tell you
decently-honestly I think your guess
is more than the breath you have left—
now I must watch your slow death
and know the guilt I feel comes to me
from you and is your gift. I have always
loved you, hated you, denied myself
to please you. But most of all, I have
bartered, placated, lied to make peace.
You, in turn, gave me your dead runes
of truth; riddles of fear, puzzles of dread—
little festers I can pick to make me think;
little scabs I can love for hiding scars.
I have always been the father, and you
the son—you wanted to steal my generation.
You wanted me old, and you, lovably young.
Your best years were wasted on the fear of death,
and now in dying you are perversely courageous.
One day I shall hate myself for writing this.

LIFESTYLE

We live out our lives in an old white Cape
and the land around us slopes to a brook
where ledges wallow like hippopotamuses in the mud
and hidden springs turn the ground to a sponge;
though we find each day monotonous as the speech
of a clock, our living here still has style:
we feather into light laughter, make plans
to break loose, dream of unexpected letters
in the mailbox, hope our son grows up,
depend on each other for courage and love;
the old calendar in the kitchen is taken down,
the new one goes up, the woodpile bakes in the sun,
nests of edibles wait in the earth,
blossoms grow wild for a crisscrossing swarm,
a universe of berries ripens on each bush;
but sometimes, and for unknown reasons,
in the stillness at noon or under the lights
in the living room or beside the windows
at dusk, one of us turns to the other
as if to say: it can't go on being this good,
something is going to happen, somehow,
somewhere, to one of us, all this is too much.

DAYS LIKE THIS

Days like this, I want to
go out and take off my clothes and put on
a cassock of dry leaves and carry
a crotched stick and get
down on my knees and give
the last rites to all the wilted dahlias
in kind Mrs. Higginson's backyard.
Then I would take off the leaves and strut naked down Main
and deliver the Gettysburg Address
to all the pigeons and squirrels in the park.
I would lean against the stone arse
of Grant's horse and shout obscenities
in the name of Eisenhower, Custer, and Clausewitz.
Then I would dance back up Main like a Nureyev,
roll in Mrs. Higginson's dahlia bed,
break the crotched stick, tear up the dry leaves,
put on my old clothes, climb Mrs. Higginson's fence,
enter my own house, and say to my wife:
"I'm home, Dear, back from my walk."

FIRST LOVE

I think of you in some suburban kitchen
with your hungry husband who was once
my best friend. Supper is nearly over
before he looks up from his busy plate,
and your eyes meet in the everyday space
that empties between you. You have become
fleshy, not hopelessly fat; your breasts
are now full, your green eyes almost ash-colored
and less bright, your dark hair is streaked
with perpetual moonlight—it would be ludicrous
to think of you in the backseat of an old Buick
and my hand under your blouse. And probably
your lips have become hard and clumsy—no longer
trained to please, they have lost the eagerness
that stirred me on the late-summer beaches
and left me breathless in the empty parking lots.
I can imagine the bruised walls of your mouth
and the shine of your teeth as you slowly torture
the remnants of boiled beef and cold potato.
A memory of your warm knees and thighs
urges me to peek under the table at your feet
and ankles and finally to where your legs disappear
into the high hem of your skirt. But you
wear scuffed slippers and slacks that bulge.
Your husband hurriedly surveys the ruins
on each plate as he folds the last slice of bread
and gulps another splash of tea. "I wonder
whatever became of him?" he suddenly asks.
I can see you looking up and into
that emptying stretch of ordinary air.
But before you can speak he says my name.
Of course your shrug will be like always—partly

disdainful and slightly staged.
Then I see you rising to clear the table,
and with that unmistakable tilt of your head—so
familiar and yet so strange—you will wash
the dirty dishes in your suburban kitchen
and stare into an emptiness that no one can change.

ANNUAL VISIT

This is the time of year my two old aunts
will reappear with bouquets of lilacs and glads,
and for hours they will waddle back and forth between
the graves. My timid aunt will read the names
and dates aloud and then translate the past.
My worldly aunt will nod or shrug and not
believe one word. Then she will wad her hankie
into her purse and reach for her chocolates.
My timid aunt will talk and water the plants
and straighten the pots. My worldly aunt will smile
and yawn. Then they will waddle to the car.
My timid aunt will be lively and confident;
and my worldly aunt, convinced that life is over,
will shake her head and appear almost lovable

JIMMY'S FATHER

When I was young
I would go over
to Jimmy's house.
I went again
years later and
I was busy
all afternoon
finding the street
where Jimmy lived.

Jimmy's father
opened the door
and shook my hand.
He hadn't changed.
He told me he
was Jimmy, and he
(Jimmy's father)
was dead. Had been
for years. For years.

He wasn't Jimmy.
Jimmy would know.
He wouldn't sit
and lie about
the things we did;
about the things
I knew we didn't
and couldn't do.

Jimmy's father
wouldn't tell me
where Jimmy lived.
he kept talking
about himself.

"NOBODY"

I think of the blonde child on the westward train.
Over and over on the midnight coach
the metronome of her words kept time with the rails.
"Nobody," she said over and over.
"Nobody." And when the lights of Topeka
flickered across her face in a bluish flame,
she leaned toward the swaying aisle of darkness,
and she said it vaguely, and finally
afraid, she pressed her body slowly back
and said it so gently, so sweetly to the train
that carried her from one darkness into the next.

THE LONG-AGO PEOPLE

The long-ago people have never been away.
They come to us from essences and aromas.
The jinni in a bottle of camphor may be grandma
back with her salves and liniments for grandpa.
Sometimes the herringbone pattern in a rag coat
can suddenly set free yesterday's dandy or gent.
Entire afternoons may be relived when we uncork
a bottle of cough syrup or peppermint. Even
the cracks in a forgotten teacup or saucer
may break down doors we thought closed forever.
No one knows what the next teaspoon measures
or what remembrances spill from a cup.
The resounding slap of a razor strap may be papa,
and a maiden aunt may still be swimming in rose water.
They all come back and wait behind the bric-a-brac.
We reach out to them lovingly at rummage sales.
We remember them with hot soda biscuits and butter.

GRANDPA

All day I've wanted
to be with Grandpa.
He's been sleeping
in the parlor. His bed
is big, and he's got powder
on his cheeks. Someone's
dumped a lot of flowers
at his feet. The lady
who wears the floppy hat
begins to sigh and eat.
Her hankie is a wad
of toilet paper. The neighbors
bring more pies and cakes.
I hope everybody leaves
when Grandpa wakes. I don't
like my stiff shirt collar
and shoes that squeak.
I can't go out today.
I've got to stand by the window
and wait. The aunt who smokes
a million cigarettes begins
to cry when a long black car
comes up the drive. Grandpa's
not going away. Someone
wants his big bed
and the flowers. I'm five.

MAUD CARPENTER

Whenever I think of Maud Carpenter alone,
I think of that place in the woods
where squirrels nutted in the noisy leaves;
where the tongue-lashing water of Denton Brook
scolded its way downhill.

                        I never threw a stone
without thinking of Maud; thinking the sky
would avalanche in sharp blue rain.
I never ate the pitted fruit without pretending
that one of Maud's accusing eyes
was buried under the pulpy juice.

How I would dread the first ice of winter—
past her house to the frog pond,
my skates on my back, I knew in my child's mind
that all the secrets of a shiver,
all the cut lips and frozen toes
were waiting behind the door at Maud Carpenter's
and would be there until the last thaw.

NELLIE IDA

Once with Nellie Ida
one magpie day—we're walking
the mud road together.
I'm wishing the yellow bonnet
of sun would stay on the day's head.
And while I'm walking,
I'm listening to the song
she sings. And I pretend
I'm holding her hand. I'm leading
her past the green uprisings
of grass. I'm trying to make
the day last. I'm holding
springtime in my hand,
and summer, an unheard, unseen bird,
hasn't got wings yet;
hasn't discovered its song.

ROBINSON'S STILL

Somewhere down on the river road
in a cloud of pines, Bud Robinson
built a still—it was Prohibition.
No one living now can recall how much
whiskey he bottled one fall and loaded
on trucks for the run south. Four dry counties
were splashed before the Feds busted
his magic waterfall. He had a way with whiskey,
people said, no impurities and smooth
to the last drop. But that made no difference.
Bud was caught and the worst drought ever set in.
All the old men who were poisoned by gin
remembered Bud's skill. There had been
no red eyes or gout reported, only
happiness and a headful of bells
when one swayed back from his still.
The old boys are now dead, and a turnpike
follows the lead-colored river that drains south.
Prohibition is over. The pines wither
in the yellowing air. There is no trace of Bud's still.
We are now being poisoned by the coughing trucks
and the bad breath of the paper mill.

THE GOAT MILKERS

No no no no, they were too far apart;
they were too headstrong together.
And so I watched them when the living
came hard; they were much further out,
angry no doubt, alone in their house
after dark. And every morning
coming down the valley for milk,
I'd always see one trailing the other.
They were going to milk the goats
and silently file back to sulk
no doubt. No no, no waving or smiling,
just walking, one behind the other.
They were much further out than they thought:
always living together without talk,
almost touching but always apart.
No no no no.

DROWNING IN THE DARK

Nobody listened, but still we heard
him raving between songs, stumbling
further out in the brush—drowning
in the dark, away from the campfire.

Poor guy, he always loved the unknown
thrills the unknown had for him.
No doubt, this made him feel unwanted
thinking of us in the warm circle

away from the black eyes of the night,
lost in song. And he, knowing
we weren't listening as he lifted
his unknown cries above all sound,

he prowled the dark thickets, afraid
and unafraid. Further out, he stumbled—
listening, shouting. Sucked under,
the darkness drove him back

bruised and bleeding. Our faces danced
in the glow. Before the third-time down
he had survived for God knows what.
But we went right on singing together.

WEDDING NIGHT

That cat-lands-on-its-feet-every-time feeling
I have one moment and lose the next—
I had it one solitary night in March.
Walking boot-high through the withered luck
of last year's clover, barking my knees
on a fence I climbed, getting wet
in the wind-whipped alders along Sucker Brook,
I found the shortcut home. Then walking
a seamstress path of pine needles, thinking
of Patsy Killibrew's wedding dance, knowing
I had ushered the last of my loves,
I came to an uprooted elm—poor, flat,
ungainly girl. While looking up to see how full
the Big and Little Dippers were that wedding night,
I wondered if Patsy would have recognized herself.
Would Patsy get wet in the alder thicket,
walk a seamstress path, and look at the stars?
I felt the same uplifting, thin elation
that alders must feel; the same mud-red tensions
that pulled at the bottom of muddy Sucker Brook.
I knew I could thread a needle of pine;
kick that flat, ungainly one to her feet.

CLARA MAPLETON

I remember Clara Mapleton
as the boisterous one who rang
doorbells after dark and telephoned
people at all hours—she would
pretend there was something
wrong in the next house.

Years later, I met Clara—she was
walking home with groceries
bulging in her heavy arms.
There wasn't much pretending done
as she stood there in the street.

But what surprised me more
than terror locked in and not
let out until dark was
Clara Mapleton, now Cranston—
she couldn't stop for long, and no,
it wasn't necessary to carry her bundles
because...because....

        And that boisterous
doorbell ringer and telephoner
looked anxiously away. Her glances
mapped the terrible pavements.
In every house the lights were on.

PETER WEBB AND THE GENERAL

That wooden-Indian expression
on Peter Webb's lacquered face—
the day he came back to Fort Devens
from Camp Crowder with Company H—
had a Mount Rushmore coldness.
And Peter Webb, parading with eyes right,
stared through the brigadier.
But in the general's policed-up mind,
the one-star thought was this:
these men are mine—one face, one force.
And Peter Webb went unnoticed.
What the general knew he kept to himself
by not looking, and what Webb saw,
Webb took for granted by looking through.

SIXTEEN

He's both fish
out of water and fowl
in the pot and he's easily
hurt. He wants to be
left alone, and he feels
left out. He doesn't respond
when spoken to, and he
blames you. He hates
conformity in others, but he
wants to belong. He looks like
a criminal with his collar
up and his head
down. He's a prisoner
in his own room—the curtains
drawn and the radio
on. You're not going
to crack the shell
he lives in. The world
is a put-on, he thinks.
Sixteen is hell.

BUTCHER

The door
of his shop opens
with a sigh as he straightens
his blossoming apron. His knife
becomes a poised baton.
He sways into the composition
of flesh and bone. Flies
accompany him as he whistles
Red River Valley. He smiles
as he shades the headcheese
with parsley. Buttons
of gristle roll from his shirt.
The cleavers of his eyelids
are raised above his chopping block
of sight. The closing door
slices the last flank
of sunlight as he pushes
a rose into the mouth of
the grinder.

BODY JOB

They tore me down and flushed
my insides. Keeping
my eyes, I watched them steal
my legs. When one of them
cut himself, I stood
helplessly on my bones,
pretending to be dumb.
In my skull I kept
a memory of legs.
My thoughts were scattered
before me like keys,
and they walked on them
trying to open me.
All afternoon I felt them pulling,
pushing, holding me up.
Their hard hands fingered
the tissues of old wounds.
At dusk by the window
my chest was taken.
The cut moon rose
in the patched sky. It was then
I saw the soaked parts
humped like islands
on the floor. In the moonlight
they looked deserted without me.
Even then I wanted
to be whole in pieces.

ELEGY FOR A MERCHANT

You are as close to me now
as you were then, years back,
when the news came—the morning
you went upstairs over
your store, and like a sweet-
toothed child, stuffed the licorice
end of a shotgun into
your mouth. I still see you
in that small room, your shadow
squashed like a chocolate
on the wall, and in the window
a big scoop of vanilla
where the sun lay frozen on
the cone of an elm. That scene
is still so everyday
to picture, so ordinary
to imagine, not hideous
at all. I can see you
rummaging in a nickel
bag of tricks for a whistle
and finding instead the gum-
drop tip of your finger
stuck to that trigger you
pulled. Now, as I look
hungrily at the toffee-
pull of years that somehow
must be stretched endlessly
to make sense, your strange courage,
cold as a Popsicle, sharp
as peppermint, is clearer

now than then. I still think of you
whenever I laugh at my own
mistakes; whenever I place
my hands like pastry on a table.

SPARK PLUGS

First he broke into
our house and stole
some spark plugs and when
we asked why he said
he was hungry. OK
this time, we said, but better
not let your stomach coax
your head. Then when
he gulped the last of
our goldfish (solemnly
explaining that he was poor)
we said, look Buddy, if you
need money, tell us—what
are neighbors for? So we chose
to ignore the gnawed roses,
even the smell of pansies
on his breath, but when some lilacs
came up missing, we said,
please eat dandelions instead.
Not good enough, he insisted,
and for revenge, he smashed
our front windows to let the rain in.
What is this madness, we shouted,
why do all this? Because of
the spark plugs, he said.

STRANGE BROTHER

A man came out at sunset in a boat,
and rowing where the rapids are he stopped
beside me. There was something about his face
that seemed familiar. Where the water chopped
the pointed rocks, I saw his rod lay catgut
monotonously over the rubbed trace
of whitecaps. Silently, we fished together.
The intimate gestures of his arm and mine
were similar. A likeness in the twilight
narrowed the distance between our boats. My line
approximated his long cast, and the slight
turn of my wrist matched his. A parallel
of leaders snaked through the water and out again.
Twin heads and tails pulled from a wrinkled sky
agreed and were killed. There, where the day fell,
mangling itself upon that hill and to die,
the sun's last blood reflected on the gills.
The echoing oarlocks were exact. The doubled
images of heads and shoulders slumped;
for somewhere in the telling waters a troubled
mutation of myself fought to be still,
as that strange brother's fought ten feet from my boat,
there in the twilight, under the battered hill.

SELF-SKETCH

Don't say I play the fool
and then pretend I'm Caesar.
It's true, in photographs
I'm pompous subject matter.
But tear the background down
and vignette my pose, I'm just
a conscientious peasant
wearing my Sunday clothes.

Study the cheap agates.
Notice the nose. Follow
the scar dividing the brow.
Here is your emperor. Consider.
Where is the man going?
What must he do? Of course
he poses. Plays imposter.
But this is no Caesar.

It's me, me, me. Then the one-eyed
camera, pretending to know,
sees only the fool. And people
will say: "Just look at him!
He thinks he's got the sky
on his back!" I won't tell them
it's true, and how heavy
the world is under my feet.

JANUARY

I rise from the soft linen
of sleep to find
it's colder.
      January
is stitched to
February on a quilt
of snow, and it will
be weeks before
the threadbare seams
of crust are torn
to shreds.
      Even
last night's wind couldn't
unravel the hem
of icicles along the eaves
or flatten the rumpled blankets
of snowdrifts.
      A daub
of dirty cotton sticks
to the sky, and a tapestry
of frost hangs
in the window.
      I can tell
by the embroidery of
my breath the cold
is here to stay. I must
get dressed.
      There will
be only a small piece
of red lint in
the thermometer today.

BEYOND THE PANTHER

Beyond the panther back
of any morning there is
a land you've never seen
and a way to do the biggest
things and to live by them.
And in one place, one man
can follow the years that come
to him, and be content
with them. And then there is
the man who wants to ride
the panther. He doesn't stay
in one place, but he would be
the first to tell you where
the smallest things are hidden.

HATTIE FARRINGTON

There was always a songbird
swaying on a heavy-
footed tree; always
the heartbeat of
a banging door that kept
some house alive
all night.

And there was
Hattie Farrington—a feather
drifting with the breeze;
drifting through the ironworks
of another battered day.

Now when a songbird
huddles on a bough,
and the immigrant wind
with its alien tongue coaxes
the bird to drop
a feather,

we think of
Hattie Farrington and say:
the softness of a feather
on the new snow was truly
Hattie's way. Bless
the shape of this morning.

SOMERSAULTS

Somersaults
I made when the clouds
were mine—my feet
had cushions as I
stepped high. I turned
at the top, unwound
like twine; the world
was a ball I could bounce
to the sky.

    Grass was
a heaven I brushed
with my hands, and air
a mountain I learned
to climb. I had
the magic a boy demands
when I went on my walks
heedless of time.

    The world
still topples, but love
for the spill requires
a courage I left
on the ground. If the earth
should fall, it is not mine
to will. I am
still taking walks
but my feet are bound.

THE PROFESSIONAL

When he was young he wanted to become
a professional rainbow chaser. Someone
who could run beyond the drenched hills
to where the sky shouldered its sack
of rain. It was his dream to find
some hidden place where leprechauns
slept by a pot of gold. But grown-up laughter
and the fear of getting lost led him
to the aviation of birds. His plucked wings
flapped in the mow as his landings
trampled hay and he soon collapsed
his mother's only umbrella. Bed without supper
caused him to dream of new endeavors; choices
one makes to learn. He decided then
to become a professional runaway—
someday. Throughout adolescence
the urge to be, to create, followed him:
rainmaker, dew-jeweler, leaf-tinter.
He grew up waiting to become someone.
Then one day he strung some words
into a line and everything he ever wanted
rose to meet him. Now, after years
of pain, frustration and failure,
people are calling this professional
rainbow-chasing, swallow-diving runner
who goes everywhere *poet*. And he believes them.

THE REMEDIES

I was purged early:
salts when my cheeks
were red, oils when I
looked pale. My lungs
were scoured with eucalyptus,
and poultices of mustard
burned my cough. I spent
my nights under
the voodoo of liniments—
bag balm was always
being rubbed into a leg
or caked along an arm.
A lasso of scarlet thread
was drawn twice around my neck
to slow the drippings
when my nose bled.
And there were the elixirs
administered by parents
and grandparents in the name
of love, in the name
of warfare. Anything to
stop those germy horsemen
galloping off to tournaments
under my burning skin.

A NEW BLUE BIKE

I remember the smell of cut grass
sweetening my tattered pant cuffs
and the magic of daylight clinging
to a new blue bike. Back then
I would skim the *Lewiston Sun*
over the graveled sidewalks and watch
the papers flop like wounded pigeons
as the news of Dunkirk and the Third Reich
bannered the doorsteps. Then I
would drop my hands from the handlebars,
whistle, and pump out of sight. Only
a magician's cape of daylight is now
thrown carelessly over the cut grass,
and the *Lewiston Sun* arrives by van.
Hitler is history, and many Dunkirks have come.
But when I least expect to be trapped
by nostalgia, when I am unwilling
to daydream or to become sentimental,
a piece of sky seen in the eye
of a puddle or a bluebird plunging
from a telephone line reminds me
that once there was a time
when a new blue bike was mine.

SUGAR AND SPICE

Thinking of the sugar
and spice ingredients
of girls that frosted the Bible-
school lawn, and watching
the hired girl through the cat's
pupil in the Christian
door—I remember how
one Sunday's coaxing got
a cousin of mine behind
the woodshed. The fumbling
I have long since forgotten,
but even to this day
I can remember the sphinx-
like expression on
my mother's face, and how
she whipped us with a stick
that didn't stop trembling
until it broke to pieces
in her beautiful hands.

PEDDLERS

The man who sold buttons
and threads walked the mud roads
when the birds were building their nests.
This was back in the thirties,
down on the farm. And the man
who bought rags returned
in early May—he was followed
by the brush man, the itinerant preacher,
and the toilet cleaner. In June,
the wandering cobbler appeared,
and the hatter arrived with the hay.
Then came the bouncy seller
of sarsaparilla, the lame allergist
who read palms, the feather merchant,
and the painter of barns. The distiller
of applejack clattered into the yard
on his cart as the apples were being picked.
They always knew what was done or needed;
they came until it snowed: the drifter
who sold blankets and earmuffs during
the first frost, the man with liniments,
the blacksmith, the mender of sleds,
the peddler who had cough drops and peppermints.

TUB AND WASHBOARD

A scene remembered
from my childhood:
a woman is
standing at a tub
and washboard—she is
singing an old song.
The gray in her
long hair reminds me
of willows; willows
hanging in fog
by a stream. A woman
who is rubbing stains—
sweat from an old shirt.
I see her hands
at the yellow washboard.
I look at the chapped sky.
It is morning and summer.
Streets are watered early
to keep the dust down.
She rubs and sings.

DEXTERITY AND COMMON SENSE

Dexterity and common sense
impressed my people more than silver.
"You're only worth as much as your fingers
and the good head upon your shoulders."
That's what my cliché-tormented people
would say. And I grew up fumbling
in my pockets for pieces of tinfoil
and crepe paper. When I was eight,
I hammered a whole keg of spikes
into the stable floor. I must
have been eleven when I butchered
a watch for its gold. Such practices
disturbed the Solomon composure
of my elders. "The boy's wishbone
is where his backbone should be;
see how the gold slips from his fingers!"
That's what my people said. The stable
now rests with a bonnet of spikes
in the uncut grass, and I've kept a watch
for my children's destructive impulses.
I'm wondering what they'll do with their lives.

THE SHACK

Whenever the wind is blowing
and everyone is asleep,
I get thinking I'm inside
an animal. Next morning
I see there are no new
tracks in the clotted snow.
I wasn't carried off
in the belly of the beast.
Mama and Papa are bunched
before the table, and a puddle
of noses steams by the stove.
But Papa, he doesn't stop
talking about the big
houses chained to the hill—
nothing but pets, he tells us.
He doesn't think the world
is getting hungrier
by the minute; he doesn't know
that we've been swallowed whole.

THE CLIFF

Every morning
I say
my poems to the cliff

then follow
the footpath
up the hill to buy

cigarettes and
bread
and sometimes wine

and every morning
the wind says
her poems to the cliff

and the gulls—
the gulls hold out
their beautiful wings.

WAY BACK IN THE COUNTRY WERE I WAS BORN

Way back in the country where I was born
people didn't care if things remained the same—
the Bible got read and the laundry stayed in the rain.
No one seemed to mind how mad the world became.
Back there, women would pin the washing to a sagging line,
and old men would thumb the almanac for the weather.
No one noticed the world as it crawled in on all four sores.
Back there, people didn't hear its pitiful whine.

WHEN HE WAS YOUNG

When he was young they placed
him gently in a nest of rags
to keep him warm in the cow barn,
and two men built a fire
to melt snow. The cattle
were restless all that night,
and great beams were creaking
in the mow. At dawn
the steaming horses pawed
the drifts. A woman screamed
between two men by the sleigh.
Everyone watched, and no
one spoke to the man
who held the icy reins.
Afterwards a woman
gave him milk and sang.
Nothing was ever said
about the poor woman
who left the warm barn
screaming. He sometimes asks
the woman who sings the same
old songs. She doesn't remember
she says. It's been too long.

UP NORTH

The panting trees will lose
their tongues when it gets cold,
and the honed grass will be
a porcupine asleep.
Up here, you won't be able
to tell the difference
between boulders and sheep.
The empty days slide past
upon a noiseless sleigh,
and from a birdless over-
cast, the flight of snow.
Up north, the mercury
gets down on its stiff knees.
Even the smoke will lay
its head upon the drifts,
and on the grates, the coals
refuse the silent wood.
Then late at night the clocks
will freeze—you wonder why
you live. This far up north
you think you hear the wind,
and it's only your lonesome breath.

THE PASSENGERS

After we eat our bread,
drink wine, and go to bed,
we want sleep to slow our breathing.
Side by side, curled under
quilts, we dream. Day after
day our lives whirl round
and round. It makes us dizzy.
Who is to blame? The wheels
must turn. The passengers
get on and hold their breath.
Each night a carriage creaks
across the dark. Mornings
we face each other wordless.
But in your eyes I read
no hesitation. The wheels
are always taking us further
and further out. When we're young
we don't mind the rocking.
Daylight touches your face.
Under the table, our child
spins until he's dizzy,
then sits on the bread crumbs.

DAISIES

When it is plucking time for my young son,
and I am Father William and wiser than words,
I won't tell the boy what I know about honeycombs.
We'll sit upstairs and talk sex;
talk about that mysterious thrill
that leaves each blood cell tall
as a sunflower. If he should mention
daisies, I'll say: "Well, there was once
an ancient theory about such things..."
then my voice will fade as if I had forgotten.
I won't tell him that saying love-
me and love-me-not is just one
way of pulling a daisy apart.
Let him learn this from some woman
who will want him to make confetti
out of every field in sight. I'll just tell him
that women are wiser than we are
when it comes to the mystery of loving,
but of daisies their knowledge is slight.

A MAN SHOULD LIE GREEN

A man should lie green
where the breast of the world
begins. He should lie
green and expectant as
a new leaf begging
for rain; green
as a weed dancing
a quadrille in a clump
of bluegrass. A man should
think green before a face-
slapped apple
falls. He should
hold each springtime
steady, the way a gully
cups its hand when water
trickles through. The beryl
of his shadow should lie
proudly before him, and he
should stand green. Each step
taken should be
chlorophyllous and light.
The time of ripening
is long for this beast,
and he is inconstant—
unfaithful to the garland
he weaves.

THE SQUALOR

Behind the dunghill where the cattle wallowed
and the ducks nested their eggs in the muck—
that place has been altered. So has the barn
where the horses switched the raisin flies;
where the bull rattled his chain and looked
with mucous eyes at the empty pail.
The squalor is gone: the carted dung is green
on the breathing hill, the mare's tail now ties
the worms, and the sculpture of the new stallion
stands heavily on its tires. One can't bring back
the squalor; can't bring back the sweating bull
swaying behind the heifer, or the red-white map
of afterbirth where the calf was standing.

MAN DRESSED IN RED

Against a background masterpiece of hemlock trees
he stood waiting for me, and I, unable to escape,
saw him mother his gun in his arms until my legs
unbuckled in the snow, and I felt my breastbone

scrape the worthless diamonds on the crust.
He looked at me with eyes I thought could pinpoint
all the ballistics of my dread with one shot—
one horrible moment to shatter my forced disguise.

Blinded by warm salt, caged in my corner,
I shook while his gunnery of sight, and jaw
locked in a grin, tempted me to turn sidewards.
I lifted my frozen chin and I smiled at him.

Sensing my fear, he shifted his gun. My shadow
appeared like a mound or a bump upon that hill,
and I stumbled toward him on the run. I was a target
caught in the sights of a love that could kill.

CARTOON

The animated rabbits munching lettuce stare
without suspicion at the hunter. There is nothing to fear
in Technicolor. One image with a wilted ear
seems to wait the inevitable foe; yet unaware

his feast will end in fire, he relishes the leaves.
Bullets riot and shake the purple wood with drama.
Panic and white smoke circle the trees. A panorama
similar to Bull Run in confusion somehow achieves

what we have never made amusing in a war:
Rabbits chasing their heads down a hill without surprise;
stuffing the holes in their fur with motion, as if exercise
had become, miraculously, the hilarious bailor

of protoplasm. The hunter in his piglike stance,
gun cocked and snout poised like a statue, sniffs the air.
He is about to embark skyward, riding the hot glare
of dynamited vengeance while the rabbits dance.

I, who snicker in the theater, wait disaster.
Oh it may come tomorrow with its crimson flashes,
with its piggy dangers and rabbit-hopeful dashes;
it may come like the laugh from the dark without a master.

MUD TIME

I'm going to walk on pins
under the pines; going
to find on a scarf of snow
the needlework of tracks.
I'm not going to play
pig on a mud road
and wallow way back.
I'd rather listen to water
giggling down a brook.
I don't want to follow
a mud road and feel
that drooling mouth of dirt.
I want to drink the maple's
milk and watch the wind
tug at the stem of chimney
smoke. I'm not going to walk
on a road that's muscled with mud.

THE SAWS

We heard the cries of those two men
caught on the saws that summer two days apart;
the moments themselves lost shape
and the day collapsed.

Young fool Moffitt's ferocious laugh
and savagery before his tears,
and Josselyn's inhuman kindness—
taking the rag of his hand with him into the yard.

And in the blindness of mercy,
among the innocent saws,
July screamed her days out on the waste of wood,
hurrying us past disaster
into September and another job.

THE BENJAMINS

Up the mud road, always
alone, the Benjamins fed
on lonesome porcupine, and all
the hidden winter they tribed round
an iron stove, gnawing gristles
and smelling of dough. But spring
trooped them out along the wall
to gawk at accidental cars
that wallowed past like hogs. The smell
of dung and greens rose on the wind's
back for miles. Yet the Benjamins,
slow-footed and sullen, heavy as bread,
had not been herded into believing
a sour wind could dance with a light step.

AGES AGO

ages ago
the wind buried
the windows with
pillows of snow
and the last stars
were hidden in
a pocket of clouds
then the thunder
of ice rose from
the lake and water
froze in the pipes
and I sat up late
looking back on
all my rages
all my regrets
as the chimney
emptied the stove
then off to bed
with misgivings
feeling helpless
and feeling low
that was last night
ages ago.

FORECAST

The bender of the rainbow is getting wet
behind the slippery hill. The sun
has no more strength than a buttercup.
The stretcher of grass is sad and uneasy—
she wants to warm her skirt before the insects come.
They are all kept waiting:
the flower folders, the ivy spreaders, the seed breakers.
There is going to be more cold weather.
They are all losing patience.
Three more months before it is summer.

DOWNPOUR

Rain crowds
the attic of
the world and slides
down its banister of
air. Clouds
crack like plaster
on the ceiling of
the sky. We can't
recall the roof of
daylight or
the chimney of
the sun. We find
sticky pearls of
mildew on
the walls. The paired
birds fly up
the wallpaper of
houses and elms.
The carpeting of
the earth is tracked
with mud. Another
end to the world
may be rising to
meet us. Another
flood. By twos
we embark.

TICKTACKTOE

When I became myself I had
to say over and over, "give
your life to a straight line, cross
here and you lose, and if you stay
you gain."

I didn't know once
what it meant to go forward.
So many lines were there to follow:
O's I made, and X's made
by others—not one connecting.

My infant son—it may have nothing
to do with this—my son reaches
and feels where his legs meet, the line
he finds beyond his straight body.
He looks at me. He is fingering
the soft flesh. He doesn't know.

GROGAN

Don't look now but
here comes the man who shakes
the grimy hands of letters
at each door. It is
our Irish postman, the ever-
faithful, conscientious
Grogan. He is a Fyodor
Dostoyevsky character.
A real Ivan Ivanovitch
fresh from his Russian landscape
via the open door of
an open book. Ivan Turgenev
would have given this peasant
a nervous disposition
and a litter of pigs. In *War
and Peace,* Grogan would
have been the hostler fetching
oats for a nobleman's horse.
In such a Tolstoyan setting
the Grogans of this world
are soon lost. And here
comes Grogan, saying good-bye
to the world's worries. We are
described in the smudged palm
of each letter.

OTHELLO UP NORTH

Brakeman Lester Emmons was the first
black man to live in our northern town.
He got along with everyone and was well liked
until he married Sam Fletcher's only daughter.
I overheard my uncle say to my mother:
"Pity their little tykes; they'll all be striped."

But Margie's three boys were born nut-brown,
and being the only black children around
they were afraid of us whites. They grew
up shy; they always stayed together—
Freddie, David and Dale. "Margie's niggers,"
Sam Fletcher said. No grandchildren of his.

Then one night young Andy Small got drunk,
stole my cousin's car, and raced through town
without a light. David and Dale were only bruised,
but Freddie was dead. "None of this
should have happened," my uncle said.
"Andy would have seen them had they been white."

SAM

There are so many things about Sam
that we don't know: something about the way
he looks at one when saying no,
the pointless shrug and the mechanical shake,
the way he fails to slit his face with a smile
for acceptance, the architecture of his brow
when he is confronted with a mistake—there may be
some rigid rule of self-control that causes Sam
to hesitate; to show no trace of surprise
in the puddles of his eyes. It's only when
the human mechanics of participation
occur to him that we get caught in the gadgetry
of his handshake. We look at him and know
that here is a stranger who lacks our social grace.
A stalled man who is silent when we speak.
It's Sam who comes up missing in the crush of words.
A man who has a blank expression on his face.

MADAM

When madam grows soft
and old and loses
control of her girls
and the whorehouse
is bulldozed into
a parking lot, madam moves
to an efficiency flat. Next morning
madam puts on her bracelets and wears
her glass beads and her lavender shawl.
In the mall she buys a universe
of tinsel stars, some candles,
a deck of cards, and a goldfish bowl
to serve as a crystal ball.
In no time, and one by one,
all the old boys who love madam
are back. Madam
sits holding an old hand
as if it were a crumpled banknote
about to disappear under her blouse.

LANDLADY

punctual as daylight she reappears in the doorway
a nosegay of compliments is thrust into my face
her bonnet tilts upon an overlapping tuft of hay
she begins to nod and sway like a sunflower
she reaches for my money and smooths the minty leaves
I explain the cumbersome realities of plumbing
a sigh of resignation climbs her trellis of breath
she mops a sprinkle of honey from her brow
I wait in her flower dump—stateless and ashamed
she transplants herself like a geranium in the best chair
then she blossoms into a garden of words

HIMSELF

Balancing on a neck that's wedged
between thick shoulders, the head
of himself rolls to the edge
but never off its perch
as he acknowledges us.

And we look back and wait
until the pushed drape of
a smile reveals a stair-
case of teeth and himself
bids us to come up from
the head-rolling streets to sit
on words.

         And afterwards,
we stand clumped in our tracks
as the shield of thin air
broadens and himself departs.

And difficult as this is
to explain—we know its true:
when this porch-wide and cornice-
high man clicks out of sight
in tiny puffs of motion,
we must crawl back into
our hollow, everyday
sacks and be ourselves.

HORNED POUTS

I remember two fishermen
shouting obscenities at the moon
while chewing off the heads
of horned pouts with their dull
jackknives.

       How marvelously serene:
calm pond, flat-bottomed boat.
Moonlight had dusted silver across
the pine groves, scattered tinsel
where the boat slit open the pond's
cool throat.

       The proportions were all
in place: moonlight had been planted,
hills draped over hills, the trees
were all in line waiting to be slaughtered,
and horned pouts were flapping
their soft bellies on the water.

RINGMORE

Two centuries back could be now—the town
is asleep. There are no faces blossoming
where the sun bounces from window to street;
there are no voices in the air
this Devonshire day. A maple, uprooted
by a sentry grave, is spilling its last leaf.
Over the cropped grass, over the crossing,
down the brick path to the empty dustbins,
a solitary leaf is tinting its way
across an English day, two centuries back.

OUT OF MIND

Next week a flat street instead of these hills.
Pancake Holland and an Amsterdam night
and the hills of Devon will be lost—out of mind.
I won't be the same man. You won't find me
walking here, watching the tide ascend.
In some new place you will find me altered—
perhaps more solemn as I climb the stairs
or hear the streetcar's imitation surf.
I won't be living by cliffs in the Lowlands.
I won't be hearing the gulls in my half sleep.

WATERCOLOR

On a brick street
I stand waiting
for the next tram.
The yellow cars
will come. Blossom
from nowhere. I'll
get on thinking:
Oh what a day!
In Holland it's
always raining.
On every street
a flower stand.
Big broad blossoms
waving good-bye.
Now it's coming:
that yellow tram
streaked with soft rain.

THE ROBOT BAND

In a honky-tonk palace where the tourists
drink cold beer, I found them on a stage
of gold: four robots playing a dead tune
for the dead guests who were traveling on
to see a tulip show. Picasso notes
hived like bees on the blue drapes above
the robot heads. No colder jazz could be had
in this cold age. I watched the drummer's eyes:
the centers were not black—they were copper screws.
And the saxophone player's lips were lips
of hose, and two red lightbulbs were his cheeks.
The bolted arms and legs kept time with me;
the dead guests swayed on their cloth stems.
We shook like cans in a room of cold beer,
and cars were streaming by for the tulip fields.

THE TRAVELER

I'm sitting in an upstairs bedroom writing a poem
and listening to the trains go up and down the tracks.
The midnight express to Amsterdam sounds hollow;
the wagon-lits to Düsseldorf vibrate my writing table.
I wish there were more lighted windows in the trains
and more passengers staring at the night.
Between the cities, I'd dust the land with gold towns
and have poets sitting in their upstairs bedrooms,
writing poems, listening to passenger trains,
and wondering how far a line of poetry travels.

AT THE SISTINE CHAPEL

A young fanatic from God knows where
(was he demented or overcome by the repetition
of his prayers?) laughed and prayed
and hungrily chewed his rosary, grape by grape.
I watched the Vatican guards as they carried him away.

Someone had said: "The Ambassador of Peru
and other dignitaries are expected to visit the chapel.
If the young man is seen, it will prove
immensely embarrassing for the ambassador."

I could not stop imagining the predicament:
would the dignitaries throw back their heads
to forecast the weather on the Sistine ceiling,
and would one of the great men ask if the beads were blessed?

The walls of the Sistine Chapel now escape me—
too much richness and my appreciation rots.
I can still see the young fanatic chewing his grapes,
and I can imagine the tight face of the ambassador,
but my only memory of Michelangelo's ceiling is a sore neck.

THE BEACH

The tourists are out with their one-eyed boxes,
and the seagulls are painting the red cliffs white.

Down by the wharf,
the girl with the long black hair
is singing a wistful song;
no one seems to notice
her psychedelic pants and her baritone voice.

No one seems to care.

All the fat mamas flesh the background
while fat papas suck their lollipop cigars;
the stench from last week's fishing fleet is in full sail;
a bubbly girl winks back at a half-blind box
and shakes her bottom at the lobster pots.

Out on the pier, a solitary seagull
is speckling a green sedan.

No one thinks of Seurat.

The sun-spanked shoulders lose their straps;
the hook of a bra is all fingers and thumbs.

No one minds that.

The bathers sit on the fat beach:
it's a lush land,
a dirty-bird painting,
a big striptease.

TOWN WHERE THE ROAD ENDS

I know of a town that ends
where the woods begin. It's solemn
and green all summer, it's jailed
by trees, and in the winter
it's church white.

       And when I
went there to stay, I said
to myself: down the long wrist
of a road you've come to live;
you will be held gently
in a cupped hand.

       But the houses
were bolted to granite foundations
and the fields were handcuffed
by walls and the people were moored
to pedestals of stone.

From a closing hand, up
a long wrist, I fled
before the fist could tighten.
Escaping one grip
I ran willingly to the next.

THIS IS JUST TO SAY

wherever you are I want to thank you
for giving me the wrong directions that day
in upstate New York

because of you
I drove north and missed the turnpike
I never would have spent the night
in St. Albans, Vermont

thank you
for setting back my life one day
because of you I found the slippery roads
through the White Mountains and the building snows
into Maine

it's true
only you made me realize
how dependent I had become on others
and how easily I could get lost on my own
I'm grateful for your carelessness or your ignorance

thank you for being there when I needed you

DESERTED HOUSE

I squat
in a purgatory
of long grass

while the rain
tunnels to the roots
of my hair.

I'm haunted
by an emptiness
I can't fill.

There is
no breath of wind
in my emptied lungs.

All I do is creak and groan
with the shifting timbers
of my bones.

My screams
have been
torn out.

My stomach
no longer rumbles
with laughter and rows.

All I hear
is the scolding snap of plaster;
plaster for rats to chew.

I can't
even open
my mouth.

I'm going
to throw myself
upon the ground

and let the world
pick up the parts
to burn.

SOUND ANY GRACE NOTE

Sound any
grace note and the melody
is mine; name
a poor monarch and I
shall set his kingdom
right. I have even
substituted for Julius Caesar
on the Ides of March.
But that was accidental—
I seldom participate if there is
pestilence or assassination.
I prefer to be the recipient
of loving mouths and hands.
I am the only man
who has served a dozen terms
as President of the United States.
All my faux pas become
inaudible; I dissolve
all my mistakes. My powers
and youthful adventures supersede
Alexander the Great's.
Rodin's *Thinker* is still
puzzling over a question
I raised. I can keep
my Napoleon image
and not go insane.

THE EARTHWORM DIGGER

He can find only
a few as they snag
the roots or unravel
in clay like pieces
of string. But where
a carpet of loam
warms the marsh, he can
loosen them quickly.
Sometimes he forgets
the earth's fabric
has a living weave—into
his bait box go
these odd ends. Some
are thick bits of yarn
and some are cut bands
of thin elastic. In winter
when a caftan of snow
dresses the lake, his catch
can be pulled free from
the ice hole. The mouth
of each fish will be
firmly stitched where the hook
runs deep. It's then
he thinks of the frayed
pieces still hanging
from that rug of dirt,
and how every spadeful
comes up threaded.

MOUSE

All morning you kept
hiding under logs
as I sawed wood.
Your nest and tunnels
were exposed to the sky.
You were on bare ground
when I stalled the chain saw.
Both your forelegs were quivering
in the sawdust, and your back
was broken. Twice, to end
your suffering, I swung
the birch hook. The first swing
missed, but the second
brought blood. Your pointed head
lost its shape, and the tiny chip
of an eye no longer gleamed
like polished obsidian
as you died waving.
I forgot you as I split
the small hill of wood.
Afterwards, I found
clots of clay with traces
of chokecherry and matted hay
in the packed sawdust.
I scuffed these under
with my foot, cleaned
the birch hook, filed
the chain saw, and followed
the path through the woods
where the injured leaves
were waving and falling.

FAIR GAME

I don't care if potatoes look
in every direction to stay alive
in their nest   I'm not ready
to imagine the suffering
of beets when their blood
sticks to my hands   oranges and lemons
may shine like the sun
but there the resemblance ends
if a cucumber should remind me
of a blind lizard   I'm not going
to be gentle and kind as I peel
its cool skin   and no
I won't be heard protesting
the plight of an onion   it can
be slow-footed and all skin
I'm not going to convince myself
that bananas resemble boats
let someone else try to float them down
a tropical river   I'm not ready
to study wet grapes like a jeweler
or stare into the crater of a cantaloupe
for seeds of pure gold   fair game
can be found wherever I am   my pleasures
have always been those of a killer.

CUPS

I have begun to notice how
my hand finds the snug crook
of their arms as I ignore
their rude yawns—their bellies
are there to be filled. The clothes
they wear insult the eye,
and when they dress plainly
they still appear vulgar.
Their chipped mouths have
a treachery of their own:
those warm lips upon my lips
soon grow cold. And when my hand
can't grasp their slippery skins,
they twist theatrically,
perversely spray, and smash
into a grotesque scattering
with every splinter poised
to cut. Then my feelings
of guilt and loss as I
pick the pieces up. I know
too well the scalding bite
of milk or the saucer
placed upon a tablecloth
like a pedestal. Lately,
I have thought of myself
beside a stream with my hands
performing a miracle. I am
lifting the gift of water
to my mouth without their help.

SLOW LIMPING

Nobody saw him, the lame man,
but still we knew he had come looking.
Across the wet snow, skirting
the fence along the stiff brook,
he must have found it slow limping.

It looked crazy: seeing one foot-
print packed solidly out of sight
and a dragged log bumping behind.
It seemed that way to us that morning
while we were standing in the snow:

we had been laughing, all crippled up
trying to run; the lame man's trail
had melted some, but not enough
to cave in the tracks of his limping.
And we stood, helplessly looking,

trying to stand straighter in the path.
We brushed off snow that stuck to us
and walked foolishly single file
all the way back. It wasn't easy.
He must have found it slow limping.

BEHIND BUILDINGS

Behind buildings there is that space
where baseballs and cans accumulate;
where the knees of the wind touch the grass,
and frost creeps in to lie down like a skunk.
In just such a place, the tomcats sleep,
and the fox-trotting mice get carelessly fat.
Beyond, the world goes on with its picked-up pace
as the peg leg rain limps through this cluttered land.
It's here the hobos come to camp
and lovers dump their hearts upon the ground.

WINTER SONG

Now I lace my boots and bundle
my shoulders in sheepskin and saddle
my head with beaver and slowly buckle
the rawhide strap.

I'm ready to straddle
drifts; eager to stand in my tracks
and to sniff the mountain air.

I'm ready
to shake hands with the wind
and to answer the telephone wires
screaming between poles.

The clothes I wear
will be my fur, and all my tracks
will be a brute's trail.

And I'll wallow
and stumble across the white paunch
of the world.

I won't look back.

THE TUMOR

A miniature doorknob
of flesh buffed red
by the sun with a fold
of slack skin hinged
upon a man's throat—
a benign or malignant
doorway he has learned
to live with?

> Though it
sticks out from the walls
and seems permanently
installed, he is able to
ignore it.

> He speaks
as if there were no secrets
inside, nothing for him
to fear or hide.

> No one
will ever unlock this deformity
or pass beyond the plumb
and watertight construction
to prowl the flesh within.

He may at times sense
its presence, but he
wears it as if it were

some misplaced finger or toe.

Perhaps a trick, or the freak
behavior of cells seeking
revenge.

       If this door
could be unlocked, the tumor
swung back, opening a crack, revealing
a danger, a flaw, my fear
or his lack,

       would he
be surprised? Concerned?
Would I be content?

I think of this whenever
I look at him; whenever
I worry about myself.

UNDER THE SKIN

Just under the skin I've lived a lot;
lived with my pulses, felt my own heart.
Just under the skin my hands perform—
I notice the muscles that knot my arm.
Just under, under the sweat, I stand up tall—
just feel these fingers that rub together.
Under the skin my fists are doubled;
under the skin the cords are tied.
I'm tied together, just under, under the skin.

FLOYD

When Floyd talked about God at Mac's Garage,
the Almighty resembled some machine mechanics
      could take apart.
If you knew engines better than most,
you had that saintliness Floyd wheezed about.
After plugs, grease, gas and oil,
he spoke of the differential, clutch and coil—
God Almighty stripped down, scattered over the floor
      at Mac's.
And Floyd, sitting on a Buick seat outside,
would smile as the boys pumped the juices of life
into the mouths of his beautiful friends.
Floyd would rave and mumble predictions.
Then he would chuckle as he studied his world of tin.

ALEX

I knew Alex Goldsmith
when he was old. Laughter
didn't crease the leather
of his face. His eyes
and light-blue lips
were his credentials of wit.
A hackmatack would best
describe his soul. Rooted
to earth he lived in a climate
of autumn. Trees were slowly
uprooted around him.
The smell of snow was in
the air when I knew him,
and often we laughed together
because he liked me.

THE UNCLE

He sits in a stuffed chair
and tries to hide a penny
in his thin hair as two
young girls begin to squeal
and pinch his knees. There was
a time he thought such things
could never happen. And now
he's not even shocked when their bodies
interlock and he feels the thin chains
of their arms around him.
He's only their uncle. An old bear
of stains and smells. He's circled
at the chain's length and he knows
the circle well. But what
he doesn't know is there.
A lifetime of familiar ties
has left him callous and only
worldly-wise—there is no finesse,
no eagerness beyond his wish
to please. Love is like
the ashes in his pipe. He quickly stands,
shifts them recklessly on his chest,
and like the wounded bear
he is, laughingly hurries them to bed.

FANNY DECKER

There were too many warts
in her church of the stump, but she
believed, and this was enough
for us to blame her, to look
suspiciously at the moon.
We didn't miss that witch
who died believing the hound's
uneasy cry. But when
the empty rocking chairs
were sent rocking, and when
the Sunday wash was on
the Monday line, a few
of her survivors still looked
at us. We didn't tell them
the world had changed in the cracked
looking glass of our eyes.

THE OLD ONE-EYED PUSS

The old one-eyed puss
out in the barn is wearing
a medallion of cobwebs
and a silver pendant made
from a moth's wing. Unable
to field a low-flying bird
or corner a rat, he rummages
among the barn boards until
he finds an upended beetle
or a slow procession of ants.
Since he has lost his alertness
and artistry for the kill,
he becomes a connoisseur
of every glittering, easily trapped
chewable thing. All the bright
candle-eyed cats around
look down on him: they arch
their sleek backs and pounce
at his blind side. They have
no use for this aging puss
with spiders on his breath.
But he responds to their prejudice
with all the dignity
of an indifferent tom—as if
he had other commitments
awaiting him. He shakes his fur,
straightens his kinky tail.
And off he goes, out where
the silver pendants grow
among the tedium of flies.

OUTSIDE

He says he has as much
as he can stand. If there
were more; more time to be
himself; more love to give
to son and wife, he'd find
it meaningless to live
in that stone house. It's night.
Another day has slipped
to sea—reversing the tide.
His wife is asleep. In a dream
his son cries. Something
outside wants to come in.
He says it's the wind, but he knows
it isn't. He tells his wife
it hurts him to be happy.
She doesn't know that some-
thing wants to come in
from outside. It's dark
out there, and he's lonely.

SNAPSHOT OF UNCLES AND AUNTS

Here is a snapshot of uncles and aunts
under a rusting sky. The spill of
sunlight settling on the grill of a Buick
blurs the face of the uncle with the cane—
he died a year after this picture was taken.
A stillness in the hydrangeas has caught
the eye of the portly uncle who is pulling
his suspenders. His look of dismay
is not for the camera—diseases
have taken over. And the aunt
who wears the fur piece will live
to be ninety. The other uncle
scowls at the witless lens; a lens
that measures the moment to wink at him.
Then the two aunts with their heads down
and their arms crossed in fat knots—
they must be thinking of bygone days;
they look so defenseless together.
It's a nineteen-fifty summer's afternoon.
They lean into the picture's center
while the stiff trees behind them
are thick with stalled branches and leaves.

THE OLD DRUNK

The old drunk shrugs
his round shoulders and measures
the street. The trees sway
obediently as he waves
the sword of a finger
and prepares the breeze
for its bivouac in a battalion
of red leaves. The tongue
of his shirttail licks
at his belt and he staggers
and straightens himself. A chewed
toothpick clings to the bottom
slope of his lip as he surveys
the injured sunset with its loose
bandage of clouds. He will soon
be stroking some friendly lamppost
or joining a choir of telephone wires
as the autumn air ripens his face.
His cockeyed stare reduces
the evening shadows to ash.
The whiskey on his breath
is the cure for every sadness
and every ill—if he should
hear the lonesome whispers
of his unlaced boots, he
will answer back. Later,
he will wet himself
and scold the reckless world
for its swaying and shoving.

CABIN FEVER

Your watch runs
down as the out-
of-breath wind prowls
for bare ground and your
stove has decided
to sleep with a log
in its mouth and your
bedroom window has
a beard of ice.
You tell yourself
that soon the birds
will perch on the thin-
wristed limbs and the ghost
of last night's snow
will haunt the roots
of bending trees.
But you have lived
too long in cold
weather to believe
that spring will set
you free, that you
will get out of
your house, or rise
from your lethargy.

THE HILL

One night a hill went to sleep under the stars,
and the next morning when the hill got up
with the sun there were a hundred stone houses
leeched to the hill's brown back.

        The hill was too round
to brush the leeches away, too round to scratch.
All day long the hill sat in the sun and frowned
at the crab sea that nipped at its toes.

That night the same stars came out, and the wind
jumped from the cliffs. But that night the wind
didn't laugh. The sea made funny noises,
and the gulls clung to the rocks.

        When the sun opened
the door of light the next morning, the leeches
were still there on the hump, and there were
brambles and late blossoms. There were even
a few berries. But the soul of the hill had departed.

AS ALWAYS

or so it often seems
when someone I care for dies,
it rains and the usual
happens. I begin
to imagine a disease,
and things insanely important
get neglected. I open
doors to presences so
clearly felt a heavy sigh
escapes me. Days after,
and for no known reason,
the straw speech of a broom
is comforting. I am
amazed and self-conscious
when spoken to; I am
twisted by replies. And always
it is raining or someone I know
hurts himself.

DECEMBER

December is when
the leaves are dead
and the freeze begins.
It's when the moon
unbuttons its vest
of stars as a shirt-
tail of clouds flaps
in the wind.

This is
the month when
the windows glow
like prowling toms;
when the door latches rattle
into speech.

December
is when the flames
in a stove unwrap
a gift of birch;
when a lonesome dog
begins to bark,
and someone going home
is cold and walks alone.

THE TOOLSHED

Now I put on my singing robes and chant
new songs—I mean I'm in my rag coat
out here in the toolshed.

Around me on the walls, discarded hoes
and shovels. This seems to be the right place
to stack my elbows on the table.

I've got four candles and a ballpoint pen,
and I'm happy to be here; happy to sit
on a hard chair in the cold.

OLD SONG

Nobody knows
just how it goes.
That's the trouble
with an old song.
I hear myself
singing it through,
but the words are
wrong. Nobody
will ever know
the way it was.
And all the songs
are like the words
that fell away—
away from me.
It hurts me now:
just knowing I've
got an old song
buried in me.

ELEGY FOR A BASTARD BROTHER

Somewhere in the mix-up of flesh and blood
you were born full grown when I was twenty-one.
I didn't think of you as someone living—
you were an apparition in our skeletal closet.
But I began to find traces of your presence
in the flinty pupils of my mother's eyes
as she stirred her cauldron of memories
and spoke of our father's excesses and lies.
Finally, you became a witness of unfaithfulness,
though my mother insisted that you were blameless.
One night you spoke to me in a dream,
and the door of the closet was open like a womb.
I never mentioned your name, never said James,
but I would sometimes imagine your face
haunting my face as I searched for resemblances
in the bold world of a mirror. Adulthood,
marriage, the birth of my son—these kept you hidden.
Before our father died I wanted to tell you
how tolerance sweetened his well-lived face.
I don't know why I never tried to find you;
why I waited until it was too late.
The news of your death left me featureless.
You weren't even old—just someone called James.

GREAT-GRANDMOTHER CATHARINE

Grandfather always said
his mother was a no-
nonsense woman; never known
to be frivolous, maddeningly
exact, and puritanical.

Father called her a bitch.
Her appetite for scandal
was insatiable; her slyness
was immense. He said
she led her eight bedeviled children
a witches' dance.

                    Aunt Helen
compared her to New England
granite. Helen thought a mountain
of rock had to be hauled
from the wilderness when God
decided to raise Catharine's
fortress of perseverance
and courage.

                    Cousin Ed
remembered her kindness;
Uncle Mearl saved her poems
for me to save; her few
surviving neighbors spoke
longingly of her cheeses and cakes;
Cousin Ethemer gave me

her photograph to keep.

                    I once
had that portrait hanging in
a conspicuous place. Daily,
I saw the quarried hatred
in those disapproving eyes.
I tried to imagine kindness
warming that bygone face.

And that New England storm
still trapped behind her brow
puzzles me—even now.
I think of her pinched mouth,
longing, no doubt, to open wide,
to scold or hurt me somehow.

THE RAGGED WORLD OF ELDERS

I first began to see my elders piece by piece;
began to measure them by coats and hats.
I saw how the day seemed tattered as they walked
and how they fell away in rags. And once
I saw sharkskin thrown over gingham
in a room the moon had stitched white—my elders.
Piece by piece I began to measure; I watched
the scene over and over; I wanted to see
the whole cloth. I didn't know why
all was unraveling in the ragged world of elders.

PURITAN BEGINNINGS

The grown-ups told him that he was bundled by angels
and brought forth kicking and screaming in a hammock
pulled by a stork; then when he asked why in the pasture
the bull kept trying to ride the humped back of the heifer,
their nursery rhyme answer seemed wise—
why not bulls, if over the moon a cow jumps high?
He trusted them, his parents, with the bees and the birds;
everything they said untied the hard knots of riddles—
he blamed the sandman for bedroom moans and sighs.
He knew the cloth on his back kept his nakedness packed,
and behind zippers his unmentionable was hidden.
About girls, their spices and confections were tested and true.
Of course he would never peek under doors or dresses.
Goodness was keeping his short trousers from slipping,
and there were things best left to the bundlers in heaven.

THE STORYTELLER'S GOD

Yes once
I had an uncle
who told stories.
And in the middle
of every tale
he ever told me
a sort of god
would rise up from
nowhere. Years now
I've kept his truth
as mine—same god
when I'm talking
to myself. Even
people I've never
met before, they
tell me how a
sort of god is
there. And right in
the middle of stories
I've never heard
before, he comes.
Just as my uncle
told me. As I
have told myself
for years.

THE ACHE TO STAY ALIVE

He came to love his first love when she hurt him,
and he left her when the pain was slight—
he kept probing his happy heartaches
and smiling cuts. With each beautiful infection
he felt at ease with the sore world.

His next love was so perfect he betrayed her;
he laughed until he cried. And she?
She wanted him until she died.
Such dog-eat-dog affairs were sweet—
they taught him tenderness.

Like most men, he wanted wealth,
a season's ticket to the ballpark,
fame, and raw meat. They gave him the swing shift
and the same routine. When he stopped caring
the world rushed back to kiss his feet.

When people near to him gave up and died,
he found it difficult to hide his thoughts.
He rocked his sighs to death and lied with tears.
Such mourning made him more alive.
The obituaries get read before the comics.

It has been this way since he can remember—
a continual mixing of pain and pleasure.
He has become an expert in such matters.
He has much knowledge of his thrashed life.
He is sick of the world, but he wants to stay.

CONFESSIONS OF AN AGING RUNNER

Because I am her father's age
not someone she expects to see
out running in shorts on a hot day
her laughter causes me to run faster
I tighten the slack flesh at my belt
brush back the wet strings of my hair
square my shoulders to smash the air
and I can feel the marbles of her eyes
rolling up and down my thick thighs—
she can never see me as I am
she can only think of me as someone
out of place in a fool's race
someone who should be resting in the shade
not angrily outrunning old age
she doesn't know I am overtaking myself
as I gulp the raw air and rush
like an aging bull stampeding.

WARM BREAD

So often I think
of a woman who
is many years dead.

I was too young
and selfish once
to know or share
her grief.

      Now I
miss her beautiful hands
and speak only
as a son can speak
and think of the things
we left unsaid.

      All this
whenever I break
into a piece of
warm bread.

THAWING OUT AFTER NEW ENGLAND

I had to get away
from my family and take
a European-Jewish wife and live
in five different countries before I found
my heart was packed
in New England ice. Because I was
brought up to dread pleasure and told
that sex was dirt, the evolution
of my love life had been slow.
I didn't become accomplished overnight.
My Semitic woman had to loosen
up her Anglo-Saxon puritanical slug
of lead by coaxing him to make love
in a lighted bedroom on a coverless bed.
Such frivolities would not occur
in a small and sexless New England town.
I'm thankful my wife wasn't born
in that land of ice people call
"beautiful New England." What would
the two of us do late at night?
I ask this because not once in my life
did I see my father kiss my mother.
They lived like straight winter oaks
swaying and crackling their branches of snow.
My only regret now is that I became
hot-blooded late in life. Lovemaking
where I come from is
sliding on thin ice,
and after it's all over you drown.

NIGHT FOG

All night the fog
runs uphill
to haunt the sure-
footed trees. The open
mouth of the valley
has an evergreen
breath, and the heart-
beat of the marsh
is bobolink steady.
The brook delivers
its long oration
as it stumbles
clumsily downhill.
Above the trees
a stampede of clouds—
stallions harnessed
with rain. Too soon
the drawn face
of daylight reappears.
There will be no more
galloping horses
when night is gone
and the fog clears.

TIMBUKTU

Same street   same faces   you get tired   you want
to leave   people know you well

You take the book down   the one you placed out
of reach   the one you say you'll never touch   never
take to turn the pages over

It's there   still there   the colored maps   the names
and then you wonder   where?   where shall I go?

Your thumb touches a river   suddenly you see   it's
something you never knew   something in you   where are
you going?

Now it's there   under your thumb   beside a river
somewhere in Africa   Burma   Greece

Some part of you that's never lived   something you
need to find   that somewhere that comes after why?
where must you go?

THE PRIVATE LIVES OF THE TOOLS

This is the land of measurements and cuts;
the world of cross-threaded nuts and sheared bolts.
It's here the awl still keeps its rapier poised,
and the adjustable wrenches, true to their multipurposes,
still have the saliva of grease about their mouths.
The snarled wig of a paintbrush soaks
in a shampoo of turpentine, and the tiptoeing nails
wait for the heavy tread of a hammer.
A bubble breaks on the watery breath of a level
as the pliers swoop like eagles on the tool rack,
and the dentures of the handsaws gleam with oil.
It's here the drills tunnel into planks and metal,
and the chisels lick shavings from the wood.
Up and down the boards and into the hard muscles
of steel these tools become sly and alert
as they travel through sawdust, grease and dirt.

TELEPHONE POLE

You're all
spine. Up
and down
a strand
of stiff
hair your
voice slides.
Your breath
is warm
and cold
air. In
a high
wind you
sigh. You've
got no
eyes. Clouds
give you
tears. Time
turns you
gray. On
one leg
you stand
for years.

THE MITCHELLS

They don't
care if
a cloud
scrapes its
back on
the sky
or a
tree wrings
its cut
hands. They
know that
fall is
here. It's
time for
them to
bank the
house, saw
and stack
the wood,
put on
their bright
bright coats
and kill
the deer.

SKIN

You do hold us in
with your blemishes and freckles
and the funny way you
zipper our scrapes and cuts.
Even your method of draping
blue-black curtains over our bruises
catches amazement. So you weren't made
to smooth old scars and wrinkles.
By aches and itches we decorate you
with salves and scratches. Belly-deep
in weight or close to the bone
you follow us all on this ride.
Up and down the slopes of our bodies,
under our armpits, between our toes,
we want your rind to surround us
with a suede tough enough to live in.

SANTA IN THE MALL

He bounces all the Alices on his Wonderland lap
as he slowly shakes his dunce's cap and whispers
chimney talk and lies about his plastic team
of reindeer. His laughter comes too quickly as he wipes
the sore of a smile from his bandaged face
and lowers his eyes to a long list of promises
he won't keep. His fat-man cheer
grows louder as he drags his empty sack
across the twinkling meadows of the mall.
Then he shakes his bent bells at all who come
to hear his archaic tales about an arctic workshop
and the dexterity of elves. Someone should give him
a new suit of clothes and barber his chin
to remind him of all the perils and woes
of twentieth-century man. His midnight sleigh
is a merchant's chariot, and his chimney stops
behind the high-stepping Dancer, Prancer, etc.
are a jet lag joke. He looks like someone
who would be emptying a stocking, not filling it full.

SWEAT

I tell you sweat is
a sacrament I've
never understood.
It's just as familiar
as bread—I've
seldom had one
without the other.

              Sweat
is an unexplored creek:
I was cutting brush
by a brook that led
nowhere. Just
under my shirt
I felt the trickle
of a galley slave's blood—
a bleeding older
than understanding.

              Sweat
can move me gently.
It's an ox's tongue
nudging the lick.
A dumb caressing.
A baptism
of the hayfield,
the stone quarry,
the slit trench.

WORLD OF THE WASTED YEARS

He rises from a bed
of twisted pillows and sheets—his tongue
a burr from the all-night beer, his clothes
a scarecrow upon a chair.

                Shirt wrinkled
like a pharaoh's chest, belt curled
like an adder, hair thicker than
a hawk's nest—he stumbles down the stairs.

A full bowl of sunlight,
a rim of clover, and new tears
of dew on his crying pant cuffs—
over the hill to the mouth of the beach
he goes.

           The world is stretching
grotesquely; stretching in circles of gold.
Eighteen years are behind him.
He tells himself he will never be old.

ONE STAYS WHERE HE IS

One stays where he is—only the landscape moves.
One learns of the intricate self by rushing into the trap:
the being aware that going somewhere never happens.
There is always the same place one comes to after the trip;
always the excitement of mapping oneself on a map.

HARD CIDER

On winter nights
the lonesome time
would come, and we
would dream of summer
and the hot sun.
Then the glitter
of hard cider—
in the lamplight
our faces would shine.
The tall pitcher
would tinkle as
we poured its glow,
and each tumbler
would listen as
we emptied our hearts

ROBIN

A baby
robin fell
from its nest.
We fed it swabs
of hamburg and egg
on a matchstick.
We watched it fly
from one hand to
the next. The baby
feathered and grew
fat. It soon
perched in our hair
and fluttered at
the windows like
a rag. One day
we took the bird
into the woods
and placed it on
a limb. A sigh
of relief sobbed
in our throats as
the robin flew out
of our lives. An
experience like this
convinces us
that life is good.

FOR WHEN YOU GO

Take the apples when you go
and take the boughs and the early shadows
that slide westward and the jeweled stain
that blazes all morning in the grass
after a night of rain.

Take the road that circles the pines—
it furrows the hill and crosses the river.
Take the sunlight on the trees
and the voices of the waterfall
and the whispers as you sink to your knees
in moss around the pool.

Take the birches, the stillness, the path
up the mountain, the uncertain doe
licking her fawn; take the twilight,
and the moments after a thrush's call.
Take them when you go.

GREAT AMERICAN SUCCESS STORY

When the young girl ran off
with the salesman from the city
he promised her broadway & clothes
& she left behind her
an angry old pa who willed
all his money to the d. a. r. &
shortly afterwards the girl
came back without the salesman
& she being lonely & big
in the belly couldn't say no
when certain overtures were made
by the scrawny & pimply boy
who worked downtown as a soda jerk.
This particular story took place
a long time ago. The girl
is now a fat matron & her husband
owns the drugstore & her episode
with the salesman was a youthful
indiscretion better forgotten than
dwelt upon. When her only offspring
asks about grandpa's money,
she tells him there never was any.
There was only the drugstore,
hard times & the great american
success story as lived & boldly
breathed by the step-pa & the off-
spring has heard all this before.

MALTESE GIRL

She is beautiful when she stands
with the trinket of her hand pinned
to the side of her raised skirt.

Is it any wonder that the people
who love her are shocked and hurt?
Six months after she has wed

her body thickens. Not yet pregnant,
she waddles from her marriage bed
like a sow to the front steps.

She hooks a string of sausages
around the handle of a pail, squats
like a mountain that has lost its lava,

and with the bubble of an arm behind
a brush, she scours her husband's footprints
from the stoop without looking up.

HOUSE OF HANG-UPS

If you peel off the skin
and shove aside the crisscross
of muscles around this back
and chest, a small child
will approach you—head
down but arms out-
stretched.

And he will take
your hand and lead you back
to where his world began:
to a woman too much in love
with a spoiled-brat man,
to a house that swallows you whole,
to a tableful of in-laws
in a bellyache of rooms.

The child
will show you the intricate mechanism
of a wrinkle and how it works
like a time bomb on a smile
or how the shrug of a shoulder
can be deadlier than a slapped
face or how the arch
of a drooping eyebrow annihilates.

And the child will lead you
to the bedsprings that chatter
in vacant rooms, to the club-
footed print of a flat-
iron in the foxglove wallpaper,

to the torn mattress,
and to the kicked Christmas tree.

There is
even a place to hide when words
become coarse and ugly.
But coaxing won't get the child
to show you this. He drops
your hand and runs off to
be there alone.

When the child
comes back, he won't even
touch you. What he wants now
is a scarf of muscles wrapped
around him and a tight
bandage of skin.

HOUSE GUESTS

It all begins
when I shake hands
and say to them
how long it's been!
Since I insist
they'll spend the night.
Next day I wait
for them to leave
but they don't go
and I pretend
how good it is
and so much fun.
Then all week long
they talk and eat.
There is so much
to do and say
I can't break in.
From pantry to
bedroom is how
a long day ends.
Finally, I
ask them to leave
but they don't hear.
I try to drag
them from the house
and all I get
is a handful
of air. When I
go outside they

lock themselves in.
They don't look up
when I rap at
windows; they don't
even come to
the door. This is
my place, I keep
shouting at them—
my house! But I'm
beginning to
think I don't live
here anymore.

THE EGOTIST'S HERE AND NOW

I remember saying to myself when standing
in a field under the noonday sun or walking
the streets of an unknown town or sitting
by a gray window at dusk: part of me
will never change; the here and now is mine
to see; this moment is caught like a cloverleaf
in a well-thumbed book.

             Then I hear myself saying
to people I meet at jetports or on freeways
in the middle of the continent or in an elevator
stalled between floors: I have shared a moment
we both will remember; when we look back
to the here and now we will think of each other;
all this we will recall.

             And I keep thinking—
more as reminder and less as conviction—when choking
on bread crumbs or bracing myself as the dentist drills
or letting my fingers worry an imaginary bunch:
I have been given the moment;
let me be grateful for what it is;
the here and now is mine to keep.

             So many times
I have found contradictions—when repeating
some meaningless cliché, lying hopelessly to myself
or appearing wise, trying to stuff the cracks
in my chipped cup of memory: the here and now

is all I have; live for the moment; there is
no future and no past.

                  Have I become myself
by watching others lose their chances;
have I hardened myself with forgetfulness
and good intentions and lies? I will
prepare myself for the moment—let it stalk me
like the stray dog it is, ready to cringe
as I turn to throw these stones of thought.

YOU DON'T GO TO NATURE

You don't go
to nature—she comes
to you so gently,
so silently through
the trees you only hear
the sound of her
invisible step upon
stirred leaves.

She moves up;
surrounds you with her musk
of bare ground—her secret
glands of dirt.

You taste
her subtle bite of air
tunneling into your throat
and out, and you savor
her concoctions of
ripe fruit, animal, root.

You can't imagine why
she brings all
her things to you.

Then one day
in her unexpected and thorough
way, she comes, and she

has nothing to give.
But by now, you are
greedy enough to take
even that, and you do.

Then her dirt
reveals itself to you
and her leaves
part and your tunnel
crumbles to dust.

All your friends
speak lovingly of you
as you are packed into
her slight cut.

          And over
you, so gently, so
silently she
comes...she goes.

THE BUCK

In the hard New England air I watched the buck die:
his hind legs palpitating with tiny leaps, his forelegs
held straight—as if he meant to break his run,
his mouth split wide with the soft pink bell
of his tongue left ringing.

His antlers were gnarled before him on the ground
like brush, his last breath became a sunset
or a flaming puff of smoke, his eyes were dulled
obsidians waiting to be buffed.

Upon the wounded leaves I let his entrails steam,
and as I ran my hand along his matted back
I felt the first stone trace of rigor mortis
pulling him into a grotesque embrace.

Then I unloaded my gun and I found the brook
where I scoured my hands and knife and a stillness
washed over me and the emptied land
as I dragged the buck back to camp.

EACH TO HIS OWN GROUND

In the high country, people
aren't casual about the ground.
They notice grass, stumps,
worms. So many times
I've seen these people
reaching down as if to hold on.
But the peat-bog people
eye the trees. Remember
storms. For them the birds
and stars get turned around—
the peat-bog people think
this true, but they won't tell
me how they know. And high
in the country where people
are rooting, holding on,
such thinking is a hoax.
Each to his own ground.

HAD I BEEN

I should have grown up in a field
with my feet pushed deep in the ground
and my hands massaging the soft back
of the wind. I should have had beet blood
or carrot skin. Had I been born
in a scuffed cradle of warm soil and dung,
I would have seen the coming of spring with all
the thoroughness of a potato; I would have danced
on the tips of my toes for the summer sun;
I would have held my breath between the weeds
and had my itches scratched with a hoe.
Had I been a bean, I would have shouted
my love with blossoms and kept my army
of children hidden. I should have had
the slender wrists of a tomato and the big dreams
of a cabbage. I should have stood proudly
in a long row. I would have been
reciting to myself had I been a stalk of corn.

CORNSTALKS

The wind will keep them gossiping
for hours. Just under, under the mud,
their sensual toes curl for the touch
of water. Before a snowfall
one can follow their tracks, down and back.
They disappear in their tattered capes,
belted with buckles of gold. They are
the pampered ones—they are spoiled brats.
On hot days they wear spinelike feathers
pinned to bonnets of blue. They appear
snobbish and high-strung. They are
unpredictable, these tall girls.

PARSNIPS

Under the snow, under layers of mud in last summer's row,
the sure hands of parsnips cling to droppings of dung—
bits of bituminous coal for the worms to mine.
And every spring when the thaw in me comes,
I reappear with spade and pail.

Down to each dirty nail
past claws still streaked with burning coal,
the lip of my spade breaks the parsnips' hold.

Once out of the ground,
their grip broken, they become sensual—
yellowing flesh warmed by the sun.

And in me
a burning: reminder and renewal of last year's sweat.
Into the pail go these limp claws as I tear loose
their tattered sleeves and fill the row back with mud.

CABBAGES

These are the hard-
headed sentries of Gurney's
militia—a squad
of ruffians in bivouac
all summer.

          Though they
meet the reveille of
the sun with their britches
rumpled and with the smell
of sauerkraut upon
their breath, they are
more soldierly than radishes
or rutabagas.

          They won't
be softened by the first
white thrust of bayoneting frost.

But they are vulnerable
in the war of hunger.
Too easily outflanked and gnawed
by marauders, they still
carry on. Heroes
every one. And versatile
as Swiss chard.

CHRYSANTHEMUMS

1.

That afternoon chrysanthemum feeling,
the one of sunburn and smoke;
the feeling you have when leaves
smother the flames;

                the feeling
you recognize when the last log
presses the coals;

the feeling of late summer—
the spanking burn along your back,
the sting of sand on your chest;

                the feeling
you have when petals escape
your thumb, and only the center
blooms red, only the coals
are left, and the feeling you have
is chrysanthemum—
                chrysanthemum.

2.

Some chrysanthemum afternoon you will see
an old woman peeling a withered orange.
Do not expect her to look at you and smile.
She will know you are there without looking up.
She will keep her head down and her hands busy.
You will not understand until afterwards.
She will make the small world of fruit smaller,
and it will be pleasant to watch her do this.
She will be a long time eating the orange.

SOME OF MY BEST FRIENDS ARE TREES

Some of my best friends are trees,
but they are always trying to
get my attention by waving
their arms in every direction
or publishing their sayings
on the well-written ground. And when
they want my pity, they play
dead all winter—finally
scabbing their bodies
with ice and screaming
as the wind nudges them
with a cold shoulder. I get
so tired seeing them stand
in one place, always hiding
their dirty toes.

       Some of
my best friends are trees,
but I wish they were
more predictable: from quiet
green to gaudy pink
clothes; from a sudden whip-
lash to a handful of
blossoms. Why can't
they be more sensible
and free? Let one
fall into a cord of rubble
and the child from that same tree
will rise majestically to block

the same view. I wish
they would sleep
like bears or go
to Florida before it snows.

TAKING CHANCES

I skidded into
the ditch. I spun
backwards until the frame
of my pickup was caught
on the frozen lip of a culvert—
ten miles from town. Ahead,
a faded lopsided sign
read: Road Discontinued.
Sleet hived the windshield
as I stepped down—bareheaded,
without an overcoat.
My shoes sponged the ground,
no jack, no log to pry loose
the truck. Sleet turned
to snow—no place to go,
nothing to do. The gas
ran out as the snow
began to drift. It was
nearly dark when a skidder
stopped in the pines.
Someone I knew. My voice
rode the wind's back.
The woodsman waved
when my headlights flashed.
He gave me coffee and siphoned
gas from the skidder's tank
and pried loose the pickup
with a rock maple pole.
I slued into the drifts
and out. Got turned
around. Thanked him

and drove back to town.
Came home late. Sat down
and wrote this poem
about taking chances.

WILTED ROSE

You with your mouth open—screaming and red,
you stand with the wrinkled leaf of one hand
on the branch of a hip. Shall I take you
from this kitchen and dump you in the trash?

No one is here to witness your rage—only
your old lover who is standing at the sink.
I am trying to think as I squint at your face.

You were beautiful yesterday and the day before.
Now you shove your thorns into the air's belly.
When the jabs go deep, there is the smell
of onion, cabbage and grease.

                         No one
will miss you, old woman, so scream if you must.
The windows have their eyes closed,
and the door has shut its mouth.

THE CATS IN THE COLOSSEUM

I saw nine of them sleeping in the sun.
They were like dead gladiators from several nations:
One was a fierce African, he wore
a helmet of battered fur; two were
Asians, they had mysterious Eastern masks
strapped firmly to their faces with tiger stripes;
three were stout Persians, they were bundled in robes
of white, off-white, and gray; two were obviously
Barbarians, dingy but very strong;
one was delicate and slight, but his proud scars
were long and overlapping like twine.

One by one they rose from the crumbling pedestals
as a half-bowl splash of sunlight leaked
from the Colosseum and drenched the hills of Rome.
Late afternoon. Time for these gladiators
to rat where the lions roared centuries back.
I watched them go. The wind rose from the throats
of a hundred entrances and became one cry.
Like rude Romans, the tourists sprinkled popcorn and pretzels
on the stained stones. The cats went deeper
into the arena, under the wheels of invisible chariots.
I stared at my imaginary emperor,
and I cheered as he pointed his thumb at the ground.
Then my blood rose along the Tiber of my veins,
and the nine brave cats disappeared into a lion's pit.
It was nearly dark when I left the Colosseum.

PENGUIN

Little priest,
one can watch you
rear you head as if
to pen a sermon or raise
your wings to form
a crucifix upon a Calvary
of snow. But who
among us is bound
by such blind faith
as you? In your place
there are no words
for grace, only
the sacrifice of fish
before an altar
of ice. If we could only
learn from you, lame
father; learn what
you preach. You are no sinner,
bigot or reprobate—
just one believer
who paddles short-
legged into the sea
and chants a litany
of hunger. Little priest,
there is no gospel
great as an ocean.

SEPTEMBER/OCTOBER

1.

September
is when the pigweeds
wallow in a long sty
of beans and the cucumbers
hide and the melons
ripen.

      I know
it won't be long before
coon droppings will pepper
the corn.

      Too soon
the witchgrass will spoil
the chard in a cauldron
of dew.

      It's almost time
for the full moon of
a pumpkin to shine
through the turquoise cloud
of a vine.

      I watch
the mustard thicken. The heartbeats
of the beets will soon
be stilled.

      It's time now
for the cauliflowers to be
big and thoughtful.

2.

October
is when the front door
begins to gnaw
on the cold belly
of the day and a leaf
spurts from the slashed wrist
of the driveway.

       I know
the birds will soon
pull anchor and the stiff-
legged rain will put on
its white boots.

       It will
be time for the fruit
to drop from the noose
of the stem; time for me
to wear a scarf
of muscles from the wood
I've split.

     The wind
begins to fumble
with the stove's damper.

I know it won't be long
before the ghost
of the old oak tree
will rise from the chimney.

CAT

The old cat sits
on the back fence.
It's getting dark—
she'll soon jump down.
Sometimes I know
she just pretends;
pretends a leaf
has fur and paws.
There's nothing bad
about that cat.
It's the design:
give a cat feet,
eyes, and a mind,
then watch it wait
and keep so still.
I love that cat;
love those killer
paws, candle eyes.
Only an eye
of daylight squints
where the sun rolls.
She's ready now.
Bless, bless us all.

LAST TREE

The day comes when I walk
to the last tree standing,
and on my way I meet
a man who says to me:
how come you use your legs
to look at the tree? So I explain
the history of locomotion:
how man advanced from horseback
to cart, carriage to Model T,
steam engine to diesel, from
Kitty Hawk to Moon Base Three.
Then I describe the forgotten art
of exercise, the pleasure of muscles
coiling under strain, the breath
stumbling from the chest, the joy
of cold sweat, and the blood's
Niagara rushing to the veins.
Such punishment is insane
the man insists, they did all this
to see a tree? Then I explain
how long ago the planet rustled
with leaves and the grass held
a mystery that no footstep
could trespass—the man sighs
as I tell him this, and then I
suggest: there was a time
when moonlight copied, line
by line, the swaying boughs;
an age when sunlight nourished
the buds to bloom; when the wind

scattered the seeds until a million-
billion trees rose majestically....
That's some story, the man says.
He can only smile and shake his head;
he doesn't believe that all those trees
are dead. Tell me more about your legs,
he says, and the rushing blood.
I want to know more about that.

ABOUT THE AUTHOR

C. J. Stevens has published poems, stories, articles, Dutch and Flemish translations, and interviews in approximately five hundred publications and more than sixty anthologies and textbooks. He is the author of *Beginnings, Circling at the Chain's Length,* and *Hang-Ups* (poetry); *Lawrence at Tregerthen* (biography); *The Next Bend in the River* and *Maine Mining Adventures* (history and adventure); *One Day with a Goat Herd* (animal behavior); and *The Folks from Greeley's Mill* (fiction). Stevens has traveled extensively and has lived in England, Ireland, Holland, Malta, and Portugal.